ISBN-13: 978-1497451216
ISBN-10: 1497451213

First published 2014 by:
Bustle & Sew
Coombe Leigh
Chillington
Kingsbridge
Devon TQ7 2LE
UK

www.bustleandsew.com

This month's issue celebrates the wonderful colours emerging in the countryside around us as daffodils, primroses and violets emerge from their winter sleep to cloak the banks and hedgerows in beautiful spring colours. This month also brings the festival of Easter - a time of celebration and renewal - and also a time for family gatherings and for making delightful items to decorate our homes.

In the following pages you'll discover flowers, bunnies, gardens and woodland creatures to stitch - and if you're making to sell you won't want to miss the third part of my "Making Money from Making" series - this month focuses on branding and packaging - with perfect timing as the new craft fair season gets underway.

Have a wonderful April - and a very happy Easter holiday too.

Helen xx

Contents

SPRING

April presents no prettier picture than that of green fields, with rustic stiles between the openings of the hedges, where old footpaths go in and out, winding along, until lost in the distance; with children scattered here and there, singly or in groups, just as the daisies are, all playing or gathering flowers.... All day long the bees are busy among the blooms, making an unceasing murmur, for April is beautiful to look upon; and if she hides her sweet face for a few hours behind the rainclouds, it is only that she may appear again peeping out through the next burst of sunshine in a veil of fresher green, through which we see the pink and white of her blooms.

Chambers Book of Days 1864

April is the month when spring really makes her presence felt. Deciduous trees produce new leaves and blossom, wild flowers such as daisies, cowslips and bluebells appear in the fields and woodlands and birds build their nests and fill the air with their song - it is in April that the first call of the cuckoo is traditionally heard here in England.

Although April is the fourth month of the year, here in the UK the tax year (or fiscal year) begins on 6 April. And as we all struggle with our tax returns, you might like to know that the reason for this goes back to the mid-18th century - predating income tax itself which was introduced as a temporary measure in 1799 to fund the Napoleonic wars. It's all to do with the change from the Julian to the Gregorian calendar in the 18th century, made by "losing" the appropriate number of days from the year in which it was adopted. In Great Britain we lost 11 days from the year 1752. At that time the financial year began on Lady Day (25 March), so in 1752 had to be eleven days later (5 April) to make the financial year 1752-53 a full 12 months long. A further adjustment was made in 1800, and for fiscal purposes the year has begun on 6 April ever since. Whoever said that accountants were not traditional sorts of people at heart?!

Filling in the tax return

4

Cottage Gardens Applique

Inspired by lines from a poem by Vita Sackville-West about the English countryside and our love of gardens and gardening….

Applique panel measuring 14" x 18" and shown here made up into a pillow/cushion cover with simple envelope closure at the back.

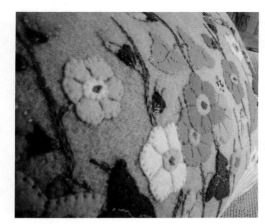

You will need:

- Medium weight non-stretchy background fabric (I used apple green thrifted woollen blanket) 1 piece 14" x 18" with an additional two pieces 14" x 12" if making pillow cover as shown in picture

- 5" x 18" rectangle green gingham

- 2 x lengths ricrac braid in green & pink each measuring 18" long

- 4" squares of wool blend felt in: Holly, apple, wood sorrel, salmon, vintage rose, baby pink, tawny rose and buttermilk (I am using colour names from my own supplier, but I have marked the colours on the diagram so you can easily see which is which)

- Embroidery floss in a selection of pinks and greens - also black, grey, red, yellow and ivory for the bumble bees and ladybirds

- Bondaweb

- Temporary fabric marker pen

Full size templates are given in reverse (for tracing onto your Bondaweb) at the end of the magazine).

Method:

- Trace the flower and leaf shapes on to the paper side of your Bondaweb and cut out roughly. (Use the colour diagram on the next page to show you which colours to cut).

- Fuse to the reverse of your felt and cut out flower and leaf shapes from the felt .

- Using the first diagram and working in sections as shown below position the felt shapes on your main fabric base. Work from the bottom upwards and when you are happy with your positioning fuse into place with a hot iron, using a cloth to protect your felt.

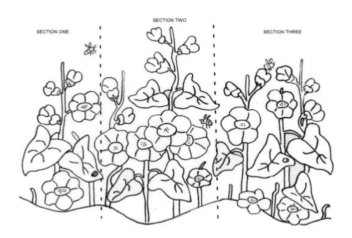

- Secure your shapes to the background fabric using straight stitches worked at right-angles to the edges of your shapes in toning shades and two strands of floss. I won't give you the exact colours that I used as it's great to be creative here and give your piece your own unique touch, but you can use the following detailed images to give you the general idea.

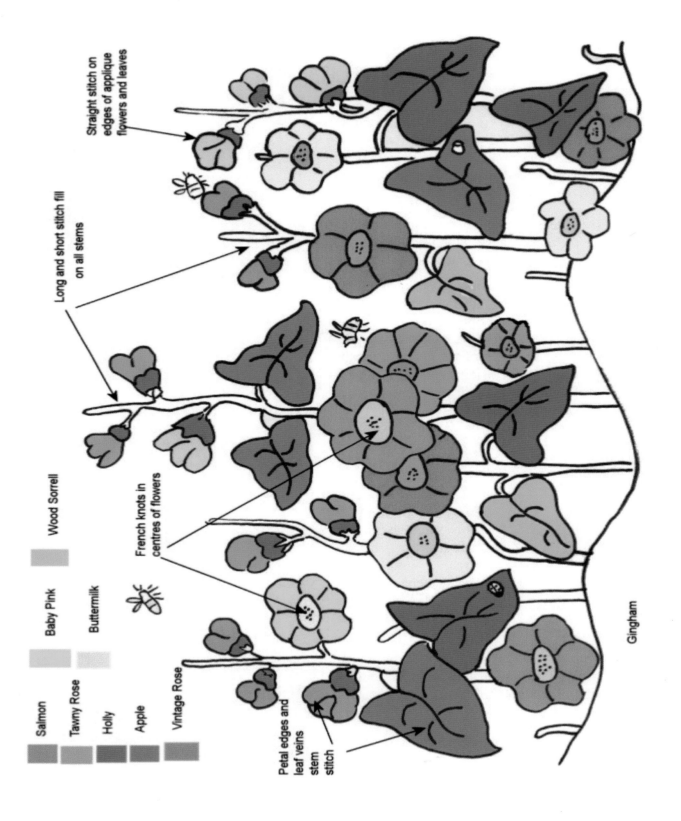

Straight stitch on edges of applique flowers and leaves

Long and short stitch fill on all stems

French knots in centres of flowers

Petal edges and leaf veins stem stitch

Salmon

Tawny Rose

Holly

Apple

Vintage Rose

Baby Pink

Buttermilk

Wood Sorrell

Gingham

7

- As you finish positioning your felt shapes in each section, using the diagrams as a guide mark in the stems, veins on leaves and petals on flowers with your temporary fabric marker pen then stitch following the colour/stitch guide on the previous page.

- The colour diagram (2) gives details of stitches used. Complete sections one and two, but when you reach section three do not sew down the bottom edges of flowers A and B as they sit on top of the gingham.

- Stitch Bumble Bees and Ladybirds positioning them on the main fabric panel as shown in diagrams. Detailed patterns are shown below:

Ladybirds:

Use a single strand of floss. Work the back in red satin stitch in two sections lengthwise. Work the head crosswise in black satin stitch. Make two stitches down the back of the ladybird for the edge of the wing cases and work 4 French knots with only one twist in each knot. Add two single twist French knots in ivory for eyes.

Bumble Bees:

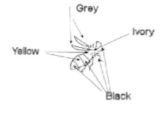

Use a single strand of floss. Work body in satin stitch as shown and legs in straight stitch. Wings are detached chain stitch.

- Take your strip of gingham fabric and cut a wavy edge. Position on the main fabric and stitch in place along top and sides using a machine zig zag.

- Position the two lengths of ric rac braid approximately 1.75" below edge of gingham and approx 1" apart. Stitch in place with straight machine stitch worked along centre of braid.

- Your applique panel is now complete. Press lightly on reverse if required.

> "All over England from Northumbrian coasts, To the wild sea-pink blown on Devon rocks, Over the merry southern gardens, over The grey-green bean-fields, round the Kentish oasts, Through the frilled spires of cottage hollyhocks, Go the big brown fat bees....."

Make up your cover:

- To make pillow/cushion cover

- Place your applique panel on a flat surface right side up. Take your two pieces of main fabric and hem one 14" edge on each panel.

- Then lay them on top of the panel right sides down, matching the unfinished side edges (14" edges) to the side edges of your main panel. They will overlap by 6" in the centre.

- Pin or tack in place then sew around the edges of the cover.

- Trim to ¼" and clip corners.

- Turn right side out and press, then insert pad.

- ENJOY!!

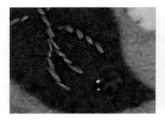

You are nearer God's heart in a garden than anywhere else on earth.

Chocolate Ganache Bunnies

Or mice ... or bears ... or any shape that takes your fancy! These delightful sweeties are all about the ganache .... a truly luxurious chocolate treat for any time of the year - no need to limit yourself to Easter!

You will need:

- 500 g (just over 16 oz) of good quality chocolate - dark or milk is fine.

- 1 cup of double (heavy) cream

- 2 tablespoons of salted butter

- Pastry brush

- Silicone mould of your choice

  (if you're in the UK I recommend siliconemoulds.co.uk who have a brilliant selection)

Method:

- Melt about 150 g (6 oz) of your chocolate and put a tablespoon or so in each mould. Brush the chocolate up the sides of the mould with your pastry brush, paying particular attention to any detailed areas to avoid air bubbles. Put in fridge to set.

- Melt the remaining chocolate in a bowl.

- Put the cream in a pan and bring to the boil. Remove from the heat immediately and pour straight onto the chocolate. Ad d the butter and keep stirring until all melted and combined.

- When the ganache is pouring consistency (but cool) pour into the chocolate shells. Any remaining ganache can be kept in the fridge or frozen for a later date.

- Place in fridge to firm up, then top each shape with more melted chocolate to seal. Chill again in the fridge to harden before releasing from the moulds.

Clotted Cream ..... Nearly as yummy as Chocolate Ganache!!

fact. If you are unfamiliar with this treat, you may not be aware that clotted cream is a silky, yellow cream with a distinctive crust on the surface. It is made by heating unpasteurized cow's milk gently and slowly. It's then left in a shallow pan for many hours which causes the cream to rise to the surface and 'clot'.

It originated here in the south west of Englan - Devon and Cornwall - and is best known as Devon cream and Cornish clotted cream. Cornish clotted cream in particular is such an important product for that area, that it was awarded a Protected Designation of Origin by the European Union in 1998. To be labelled as such, Cornish clotted cream must be made with milk produced in Cornwall. And it's actually very easy to be sure that you're consuming the genuine stuff as cows grazing in Cornwall produce a cream with a slight yellowish colour due to the carotene levels in the local grass.

I love the part of ganache making when you have to bring the cream to boiling point, and doing so often makes me think about the process of making clotted cream - one of the most heavenly foods (in my opinion at least) known to woman! Living in Devon I am in the heart of clotted cream country - so it was easy for me to do a little research and find out more about this delicious west country treat.

Mentions of clotted cream can be found throughout the folklore of south west England. In one tale from Dartmoor, a princess bathed in clotted cream in order to marry an elvish prince, thus thwarting an evil witch's attempts to prevent the marriage by souring her earlier cream baths. She was unable to sour the clotted cream and the princess happily married her elvish prince.

Clotted cream is the perfect accompaniment for a scone, some homemade jam and a nice cup of tea - the classic English cream tea in

Below is Mrs Beeton's Victorian recipe for clotted cream:

2369. In Devonshire, celebrated for its dairy system, the milk is always scalded. The milk-pans, which are of tin, and contain from 10 to 12 quarts, after standing 10 or 12 hours, are placed on a hot plate of iron, over a stove, until the cream has formed on the surface, which is indicated by the air-bubbles rising through the milk, and producing blisters on the surface-coating of cream. This indicates its approach to the boiling point: and the vessel is now removed to cool. When sufficiently, that is, quite cool, the cream is skimmed off with the slice: it is now the clouted cream for which Devonshire is so famous. It is now placed in the churn, and churned until the butter comes, which it generally does in a much shorter time than by the other process. The butter so made contains more *caseine* than butter made in the usual way, but does not keep so long.

TWO PUZZLES *devised by MARION WOOD*

ANIMALS IN THE ARK

Fill in the missing vowels to find the animals.

SOLUTION: Camel; lamb; bear; wolf; lion; tiger; monkey; zebra; goat; horse.

A WORD-SQUARE

To make the Word-Square, put the initial letters of the objects in the numbered squares.

SOLUTION: 1. Tree; 2. Owl; 3. Pear; 4. Oranges; 5. Rose; 6. Egg; 7. Pansy; 8. Ears; 9. Nest.

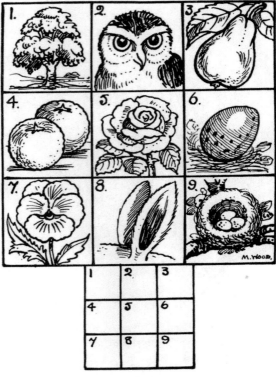

A WORD-SQUARE

Vintage Word Puzzles

I have in my possession a whole tube of vintage classroom posters inherited from my Mum, who taught very young children (ages 5 - 7) for many years. Later in the magazine you'll discover a delightful illustration for "Spring" together with a link to download a printable high-resolution version. These word puzzles appear on the reverse (along with other teaching aids) and I think the illustrations are charming. I particularly like the cleverness of the word square and think it would make a delightful stitchery - another idea to add to my rather too long list of things to do!

I do hope you enjoy these puzzles too!

Running Hare Softie

I often see brown hares in the fields above Start Bay when I take Ben and Daisy to their favourite kennels - and here's my interpretatinon of one of these beautiful animals.

Finished hare measures just under 12" from outstretched back paw to tip of front paw.

You will need:

- 12" square brown felt

- Matching stranded cotton floss - also pink floss

- Four ¾" wooden buttons

- 2 small black spherical beads

- One ¼" brown button

- Tiny scraps of pink fabric for inner ears

- Small amount of white or cream wool to make pompom for tail (or use a 1 ½"purchased pompom)

- Toy stuffing

- Strong thread.

- Long needle (helpful, but not essential)

- Wooden stand (I used one from a damaged decorative decoy bird).

Notes on making:

- Join seams with cross stitch using two strands of floss. Place pieces with wrong sides together. Work half one stitch in one direction, then return the other way to complete the stitch.

- Take your time stuffing your hare. Insert small pieces of stuffing to avoid lumpiness and push down will into the smaller areas with your stuffing stick. This is the only "specialist" tool I use and is simply a bamboo skewer with the point broken off and the end frayed so it "grabs" the stuffing when I push the tool in.

- I used an old stand from a broken decoy bird that I painted and decorated with ribbon and ric-rac braid. You could make your own with slim dowling inserted into a wooden base (or a giant spool would be nice!)

Assemble your hare:

- Cut out all pieces from template (full size). Stitch together pieces for two front and two back legs. Start in the middle bottom of each leg and work around the top, then stuff the leg before closing the final gap.

- Join the body gussets to the body pieces from C to D. Join body main pieces from D to A and gusset central seam, leaving a gap from G to F to insert the stand.

- Insert head gusset from A to B and join main body pieces along back, stuffing as you go. (The shape won't look very much like a hare at this point, the legs make all the difference).

- Stitch ear inners to main ear pieces using small straight stitches and pink floss. Fold in half at the base and attach to sides of head at E on template.

- Join legs to body with wooden buttons using strong thread. Stitch right through the body and pull fairly tightly to give some nice contours.

- Add nose and eyes and stitch pink cheeks using the photos as a guide.

- Make a small pompom with your wool and stitch in place.

- Push stand up through the hole you left in the hare's belly and stitch up any extra space.

- FINISHED!

A Day in the Mountains

Extract from "Heidi" by Joanna Spyri

Heidi was awakened early next morning by a loud whistle. Opening her eyes, she saw her little bed and the hay beside her bathed in golden sunlight. For a short while she did not know where she was, but when she heard her grandfather's deep voice outside, she remembered everything. She remembered how she had come up the mountain the day before and left old Ursula, who was always shivering with cold and sat near the stove all day. While Heidi lived with Ursula, she had always had to stay indoors so the old woman could see her. Being deaf, Ursula was afraid to let Heidi go outside, and the child had often fretted in the narrow room and had longed to run and play outside. She was therefore delighted to find herself in her new home and hardly could wait to see the goats again. Jumping out of bed, she put on her few things and in a short time went down the ladder and ran outside. Peter was already there with his flock, waiting for Schwänli and Bärli, whom the grandfather was just bringing to join the other goats.

"Do you want to go with him to the pasture?" asked the grandfather.

"Yes," cried Heidi, clapping her hands.

"Go now, and wash yourself first, for the sun will laugh at you if he sees how dirty you are. Everything is ready there for you," he added, pointing to a large tub of water that stood in the sun. Heidi did as she was told, and washed and rubbed herself till her cheeks were glowing. In the meanwhile the grandfather called to Peter to come into the hut and bring his bag along. The boy followed the old man, who commanded him to open the bag in which he carried his frugal meal. The grandfather put into the bag a piece of bread and a slice of cheese, that were easily twice as large as those the boy had in the bag himself.

"The little bowl goes in, too," said the Grandfather, "for the child does not know how to drink straight from the goat, the way you do. She is going to stay with you all day, therefore milk two bowls full for her dinner. Look out that she does not fall over the rocks! Do you hear?"

Just then Heidi came running in. "Grandfather, can the sun still laugh at me?" she asked. The child had rubbed herself so violently with the coarse towel which the grandfather had put beside the tub that her face, neck and arms were as red as a lobster. With a smile the grandfather said: "No, he can't laugh any more now; but when you come home to-night you must go into the tub like a fish. When one goes about like the goats, one gets dirty feet. Be off!"

They started merrily up the Alp. A cloudless, deep-blue sky looked down on them, for the wind had driven away every little cloud in the night. The fresh green mountain-side was bathed in brilliant sunlight, and many blue and yellow flowers had opened. Heidi was wild with joy and ran from side to side. In one place she saw big patches of fine red primroses, on another spot blue gentians

sparkled in the grass, and everywhere the golden rock-roses were nodding to her. In her delight at finding such treasures, Heidi even forgot Peter and his goats. She ran far ahead of him and then strayed away off to one side, for the sparkling flowers tempted her here and there. Picking whole bunches of them to take home with her, she put them all into her little apron.

Peter, whose round eyes could only move about slowly, had a hard time looking out for her. The goats were even worse, and only by shouting and whistling, especially by swinging his rod, could he drive them together.

"Heidi, where are you now?" he called quite angrily.

"Here," it sounded from somewhere. Peter could not see her, for she was sitting on the ground behind a little mound, which was covered with fragrant flowers. The whole air was filled with their perfume, and the child drew it in, in long breaths.

"Follow me now!" Peter called out. "The grandfather has told me to look out for you, and you must not fall over the rocks."

"Where are they?" asked Heidi without even stirring.

"Way up there, and we have still far to go. If you come quickly, we may see the eagle there and hear him shriek."

That tempted Heidi, and she came running to Peter, with her apron full of flowers.

"You have enough now," he declared. "If you pick them all to-day, there won't be any left to-morrow." Heidi admitted that, besides which she had her apron already full. From now on she stayed at Peter's side. The goats, scenting the pungent herbs, also hurried up without delay.

Peter usually made his home for the day at the foot of a high cliff, which seemed to reach far up into the sky. Overhanging rocks on one side made it dangerous, so that the grandfather was wise to warn Peter. After they had reached their destination, the boy took off his bag, putting it in a little hollow in the ground. The wind often blew in violent gusts up there, and Peter did not want to lose his precious load. Then he lay down in the sunny grass, for he was very tired.

Heidi, taking off her apron, rolled it tightly together and put it beside Peter's bag. Then, sitting down beside the boy, she looked about her. Far down she saw the glistening valley; a large field of snow rose high in front of her. Heidi sat a long time without stirring, with Peter asleep by her side and the goats climbing about between the bushes. A light breeze fanned her cheek and those big mountains about her made her feel happy as never before. She looked up at the mountain-tops till they all seemed to have faces, and soon they were familiar to her, like old friends. Suddenly she heard a loud, sharp scream, and looking up she beheld the largest bird she had ever seen, flying above her. With outspread wings he flew in large circles over Heidi's head.

"Wake up, Peter!" Heidi called. "Look up, Peter, and see the eagle there!"

Peter got wide wake, and then they both watched the bird breathlessly. It rose higher and higher into the azure, till it disappeared at last behind the mountain-peak.

"Where has it gone?" Heidi asked.

"Home to its nest," was Peter's answer.

"Oh, let's climb up there and see!" implored Heidi, but Peter, expressing decided disapproval in his voice, answered: "Oh dear, Oh dear, not even goats could climb up there! Grandfather has told me not to let you fall down the rocks, so we can't go!"

Peter now began to call loudly and to whistle, and soon all the goats were assembled on the green field. Heidi ran into their midst, for she loved to see them leaping and playing about.

Peter in the meantime was preparing dinner for Heidi and himself, by putting her large pieces on one side and his own small ones on the other. Then he milked Bärli and put the full bowl in the middle. When he was ready, he called to the little girl. But it took some time before she obeyed his call.

"Stop jumping, now," said Peter, "and sit down; your dinner is ready."

"Is this milk for me?" she inquired.

"Yes it is; those large pieces also belong to you. When you are through with the milk, I'll get you some more. After that I'll get mine."

"What milk do you get?" Heidi inquired.

"I get it from my own goat, that speckled one over there. But go ahead and eat!" Peter commanded again. Heidi obeyed, and when the bowl was empty, he filled it again. Breaking off a piece of bread for herself, she gave Peter the rest, which was still bigger than his own portion had been. She handed him also the whole slice of cheese, saying: "You can eat that, I have had enough!"

Peter was speechless with surprise, for it would have been impossible for him ever to give up any of his share. Not taking Heidi in earnest, he hesitated till she put the things on his knees. Then he saw she really meant it, and he seized his prize. Nodding his thanks to her, he ate the most wonderful meal he had ever had in all his life. Heidi was watching the goats in the meantime, and asked Peter for their names.

The boy could tell them all to her, for their names were about the only thing he had to carry in his head. She soon knew them, too, for she had listened attentively. One of them was the Big Turk, who tried to stick his big horns into all the others. Most of the goats ran away from their rough comrade. The bold Thistlefinch alone was not afraid, and running his horns three or four times into the other, so astonished the Turk with his great daring that he stood still and gave up fighting, for the Thistlefinch had sharp horns and met him in the most warlike attitude. A small, white goat, called Snowhopper, kept up a pitiful bleating, which induced Heidi to console it several times. Heidi at last went to the little thing again, and throwing her arms around its head, she asked, "What is the matter with you, Snowhopper? Why do you always cry for help?" The little goat pressed close to Heidi's side and became perfectly quiet. Peter was still eating, but between the swallows he called to Heidi: "She is so unhappy, because the old goat has left us. She was sold to somebody in Mayenfeld two days ago."

"Who was the old goat?"

"Her mother, of course."

"Where is her grandmother?"

"She hasn't any."

"And her grandfather?"

"Hasn't any either."

"Poor little Snowhopper!" said Heidi, drawing the little creature tenderly to her. "Don't grieve any more; see, I am coming up with you every day now, and if there is anything the matter, you can come to me."

Snowhopper rubbed her head against Heidi's shoulder and stopped bleating. When Peter had finally finished his dinner, he joined Heidi.

The little girl had just been observing that Schwänli and Bärli were by far the cleanest and prettiest of the goats. They evaded the obtrusive Turk with a sort of contempt and always managed to find the greenest bushes for themselves. She mentioned it to Peter, who replied: "I know! Of course they are the prettiest, because the grandfather washes them and gives them salt. He has the best stable by far."

All of a sudden Peter, who had been lying on the ground, jumped up and bounded after the goats. Heidi, knowing that something must have happened, followed him. She saw him running to a dangerous abyss on the side. Peter had noticed how the rash Thistlefinch had gone nearer and nearer to the dangerous spot. Peter only just came in time to prevent the goat from falling down over the very edge. Unfortunately Peter had stumbled over a stone in his hurry and was only able to catch the goat by one leg. The Thistlefinch, furious to find himself stopped in his tracks was bleatingd furiously. Not being able to get up, Peter loudly called for help. Heidi immediately saw that Peter was nearly pulling off the animal's leg. She quickly picked some fragrant herbs and holding them under the animal's nose, she said soothingly: "Come, come, Thistlefinch, and be sensible. You

might fall down there and break your leg. That would hurt you horribly."

The goat turned about and devoured the herbs Heidi held in her hand. When Peter got to his feet, he led back the runaway with Heidi's help. When he had the goat in safety, he raised his rod to beat it for punishment. The goat retreated shyly, for it knew what was coming. Heidi screamed loudly: "Peter, no, do not beat him! Look how scared he is."

"He well deserves it," snarled Peter, ready to strike. But Heidi, seizing his arm, shouted, full of indignation: "You mustn't hurt him! Let him go!"

Heidi's eyes were sparkling, and when he saw her with her commanding mien, he desisted and dropped his rope. "I'll let him go, if you give me a piece of your cheese again to-morrow," he said, for he wanted a compensation for his fright.

"You may have it all to-morrow and every day, because I don't need it," Heidi assured him. "I shall also give you a big piece of bread, if you promise never to beat any of the goats."

"I don't care," growled Peter, and in that way he gave his promise.

Thus the day had passed, and the sun was already sinking down behind the mountains. Sitting on the grass, Heidi looked at the bluebells and the wild roses that were shining in the last rays of the sun. The peaks also started to glow, and Heidi suddenly called to the boy: "Oh, Peter, look! everything is on fire. The mountains are burning and the sky, too. Oh, look! the moon over there is on fire, too. Do you see the mountains all in a glow? Oh, how beautiful the snow looks! Peter, the

eagle's nest is surely on fire, too. Oh, look at the fir-trees over there!"

Peter looked up and said to Heidi: "This is no fire; it always looks like that."

"But what is it then?" asked Heidi eagerly, gazing about her everywhere.

"It gets that way of itself," explained Peter.

"Oh look! Everything is all rosy now! Oh, look at this mountain over there with the snow and the sharp peaks. What is its name?"

"Mountains have no names," he answered.

"Oh, see, how beautiful! It looks as if many, many roses were growing on those cliffs. Oh, now they are getting grey. Oh

dear! the fire has gone out and it is all over. What a terrible shame!" said Heidi quite despondently.

"It will be the same again tomorrow," Peter reassured her. "Come now, we have to go home."

When Peter had called the goats together, they started downwards.

"Will it be like that every day when we are up?" asked Heidi, eagerly.

"It usually is," was the reply.

"What about tomorrow?" she inquired.

"Tomorrow it will be like that, I am sure," Peter affirmed.

That made Heidi feel happy again. She walked quietly by Peter's side, thinking over all the new things she had seen.

At last, reaching the hut, they found the grandfather waiting for them on a bench under the fir-trees. Heidi ran up to him and the two goats followed, for they knew their master. Peter called to her: "Come again tomorrow! Good-night!"

Digging the Allotment

April sees the beginning of the growing season proper and all around the village gardeners are out in force preparing their plots for the warmer months ahead.

This little bunny was designed by Flapdoodledesigns and is really simple to stitch - great for the beginner sewist or a quick project for the more experienced.

Shown mounted in a 7" hoop

when ending one stitch and beginning another. Otherwise your lines will look broken and untidy.

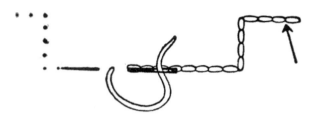

Back stitch is worked from right to left. Bring your needle out a short distance from the beginning of the line you want to stitch (see the arrow in the diagram above). Then insert it back through the fabric at the beginning of your line - effectively taking a step "back" - and bring it forward again an equal distance forward from where you first started. You are actually taking along stitch forward beneath your fabric, then a short backward stitch on the right side - joining with the previous stitch.

For more Flapdoodledesigns images please visit Jacqui's Facebook page:

https://www.facebook.com/flapdoodledesigns

You will need:

- 10" square piece of neutral pale coloured cotton, linen or cotton/linen blend fabric
- DMC stranded cotton embroidery floss in colours 310, 322, 434, 906, 907, 970, 989, 3755, 3781, 3822, 3824, blanc

Stitching notes:

The actual stitching of this piece is very simple indeed. The only stitches used are back stitch and straight stitch.

Two strands of floss are used throughout except for:

Bunny whiskers - these are a single long straight stitch in one strand of blanc floss.

Shading on bunny trousers: the black shading which is worked to the right of the vertical blue lines is a single strand of 310.

The tail is lots of straight stitches.

Although back stitch is one of the easiest stitches of all, you still need to take care and attention to work it well. Be sure to work exactly along the lines of your pattern and that your needle enters and emerges through your fabric in the same place

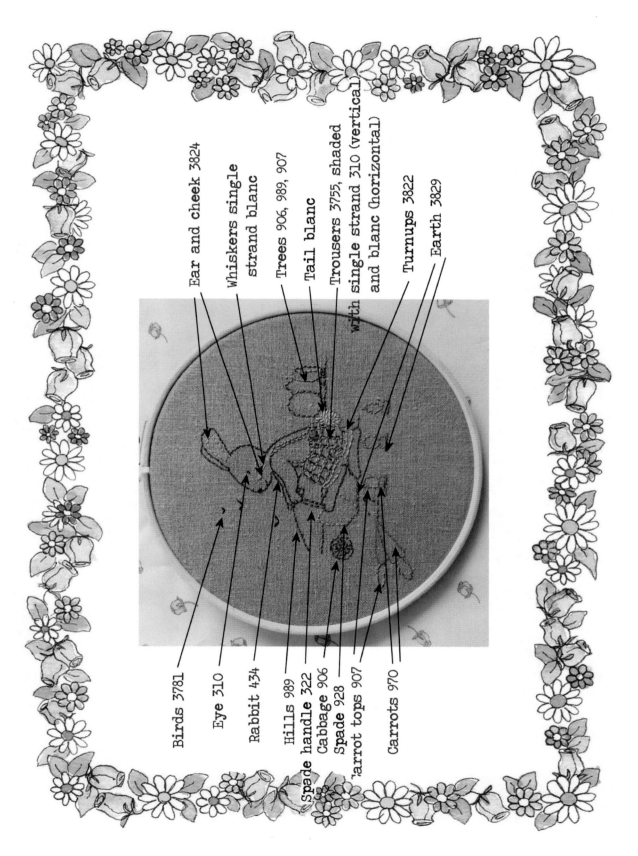

Ear and cheek 3824

Whiskers single strand blanc

Trees 906, 989, 907

Tail blanc

Trousers 3755, shaded

with single strand 310 (vertical and blanc (horizontal)

Turnups 3822

Earth 3829

Birds 3781

Eye 310

Rabbit 434

Hills 989

Spade handle 322

Cabbage 906

Spade 928

Carrot tops 907

Carrots 970

23

Stitching Simple Flower Forms

By April spring is (hopefully) well underway and the first blossoms are beginning to appear in the hedgerows - forerunners of the riot of colour and bloom that heralds May. So this month I have chosen another extract from a vintage book "The Embroidery Book" by Winifred M Clarke - all about stitching flower shapes The words are hers ....

Here are ten simple forms which suggest many ways of working a flower; and these same methods might be adapted for larger flowers as well. If the same flower shape appears in a design more than once or twice it is interesting to work it in another way. (The balance in colour and texture can always be kept the same). These simple flowers do not need to be fully describe as the illustrations suggest the stitches. However, the order in which the stitches are use in each flower might be helpful:

1. Chain stitch outline. Fill in petals. French knots in centre and one row of back stitch.

2. Buttonhole stitch outer part of petal. Couch across centre. Add French knots.

3. Long and short stitch petals. Chain stitch around base of petals. Work centre in satin stitch.

4. Chain stitch each petal. French knots around base of them. Make solid circle in centre. Three loops are added inside each petal. With small stem stitches add the points between petals.

5. Chain stitch petals. French knots at base of each one. Centre in buttonhole stitch. Add loops in petals.

6. Two rows of chain stitch decorate each petal. Buttonhole stitch forms the centre with five French knots. Add loops between petals.

7. Satin stitch solid part of petal and add outline of back stitch. French knots and back stitch form centre. Back stitch curves between petals, add French knots.

8. Chain stitch around petals and centre. Satin stitch central circle, add back stitch round it.

Simple flower forms with decorative stitches added.

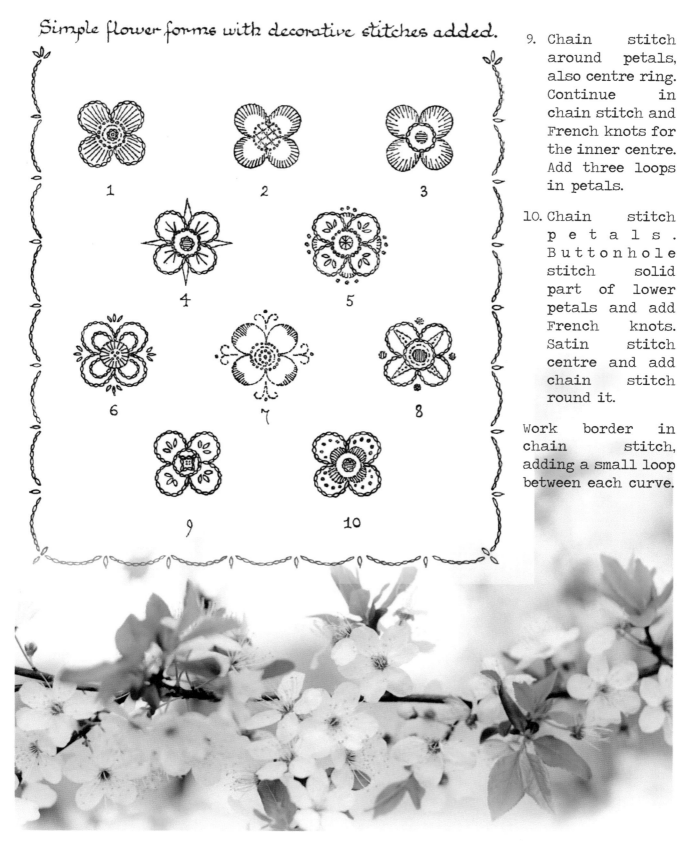

9. Chain stitch around petals, also centre ring. Continue in chain stitch and French knots for the inner centre. Add three loops in petals.

10. Chain stitch petals. Buttonhole stitch solid part of lower petals and add French knots. Satin stitch centre and add chain stitch round it.

Work border in chain stitch, adding a small loop between each curve.

Country Houses Bunting

There's bunting … and then there's Country Houses bunting - a great way to use up all your scraps and create a wonderful talking point in your home - or why not make as a special gift for somebody moving into a new house? Much nicer than a card, and lasts longer too!

Each house measures 8" tall x 6 ½" wide appro

To make a garland of eight houses

You will need:

- 8 rectangles, each measuring 7" x 9" of medium weight fabric for the house fronts

- 8 rectangles, each measuring 7" x 4" of medium or light weight fabric for the house roofs

- 8 rectangles, each measuring 7" x 9" of medium or light weight fabric for the reverse of the houses (a good moment to use up some not very interesting fabrics you may have lying around)

- Scraps of printed cotton fabrics for the windows and doors

- Scraps of pink and/or red felt for the hearts on the roofs

- Red and/or pink cotton embroidery floss

- 4 yards of 1" cotton tape (or bias binding)

- 8 small buttons for door knobs

- Bondaweb

- Embroidery foot for your sewing machine

- Dark and light coloured thread

To make each house:

- Using the full size template, cut out a house shape from your medium weight fabric and place face up on a clean flat surface.

- You will create the roof using the stitch and flip technique. Place the rectangle of roof fabric face down on top of your house shape with one edge ¼ " above the shaping for the roof.

- Pin, then stitch along the top edge with a ¼" seam allowance. Flip your roof shape up towards the top of the house and press.

- Using your main fabric piece as a guide trim the roof to shape.

- Trace the shapes for windows and door onto the paper side of your Bondaweb. Cut out roughly then fuse to the reverse of your printed cottons. Cut out shapes and position on your house using the template as a guide. Fuse into place when you're happy with their positioning.

- Cut out heart shapes from felt and fuse to the roof in the same way.

- Fit the embroidery foot to your machine and drop the feed dogs. With dark thread in your needle and a pale colour in your bobbin, stitch around the edges of the windows and doors, and the cross shapes on the windows (these extend a little way beyond the window edges for a naïve feel). Go around twice - don't try to be too neat, aim for a sort of scribbled effect. See the picture above for guidance.

- Attach the heart shape to the roof with small straight stitches in 2 strands of floss, worked at right angles to the edges of the heart shapes.

- Attach the buttons to the doors. Press your work lightly on the reverse.

- Cut out 8 house shapes from your backing fabric and join to the house fronts with right sides together. (see template for stitching guide). Leave the top of the roof open for turning. Clip corners, turn through and press on reverse.

- Trim the top of the roof so the edges of all the fabrics are absolutely straight and even.

- Decide on the order you'd like your houses and pin to the tape, folding the tape in half to enclose the raw edges at the top of the house roof. Leave a gap of about 8" between each house.

- Stitch along the folded tape to secure houses - I continue between the houses too to avoid lots of stopping and starting. You should have plenty extra at either end for hanging.

- Your bunting is now finished!

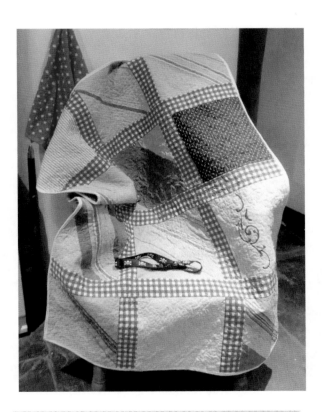

If you're unfamiliar with stitch'n'flip, then please take a look at my free tutorial (featuring Ben's birthday topper!).

http://bustleandsew.com/freepatterns/Stitchnfliptute.pdf

Making Money from Making

It's wonderful when you discover that it's actually possible to earn some money by doing something you love - like sewing! Over the next few issues I'm offering you some hints and tips on successfully selling the items you love to make. This week branding and packaging....

New entrepreneurs don't always appreciate the power of branding - and how hard good, effective branding will work for their business. Consider the giant company Coca-Cola - their brand is instantly recognised across the globe - the red and white colours and swirly font communicate the same message whether you can actually read the text or not. Coca-Cola themselves are totally aware of the importance of their branding - consider the following quote from one of their executives:

"If Coca-Cola were to lose all of its production-related assets in a disaster, the company would survive. By contrast, if all consumers were to have a sudden lapse of memory and forget everything related to Coca-Cola, the company would go out of business."

The first question to ask yourself is - do you completely understand what branding is, and how it can help your business? Branding is a way of communicating your business's values and standards to your potential customers. Your business can benefit enormously if you are able to create a brand that presents it as trustworthy, unique, exciting, value for money - or whatever you feel is appropriate. You will do this through effectively using design elements, advertising, marketing, etc to communicate clearly what your business stands for.

The key to building a successful brand is to take into account every aspect of your business, ensuring you choose colours, styles and themes that lend themselves to being used throughout your business in a consistent manner, especially if you intend to market your work online, including social media - and also if you intend to sell at craft fairs.

To summarise then, your brand is your promise to your customer. It tells them what they can expect from your products and services. A successful brand makes your business distinctive and helps it stand out amongst the competition. Your brand is created from who you are, what you want your business to be and who (and what) your potential customers perceive you and your to be.

When you are developing a brand for your business there are some basic questions you should ask yourself - some you will need to think about - and others, I am sure, you will be able to answer instantly:

What image do I want my business to portray? Am I cute, modern, vintage-inspired etc Who is my target market? What do they like, want and need from my business? What is my USP* ? What is my business personality, and how do I convey this to my customers? Who are my competition - will my brand stand out in what may be a crowded marketplace? What is my strapline - and will people know what my business offers from it?

At Bustle & Sew I restrict my header and logo to the little Bustle & Sew bunny, with two main colours (teal and burgundy) and use just two fonts. This ensures consistency across all the places Bustle & Sew has a presence, and helps brand recognition. My little bunny communicates, I hope, that Bustle & Sew is a friendly sort of place, perhaps a little old-fashioned even, but one where it's fun to hang out. Bustle & Sew's strapline is "Love to Sew … and Sew with Love" which I hope encapsulates what my business is all about.

Your logo is a vitally important part of your business branding, so if you're not a graphic designer, or not confident creating your own design, then it's worth paying for some professional help.

Your fonts are also crucial to the feel of your brand. It's also very important that they're easy to read - so make sure that any text is large enough and contrasts well with your background colours. Try to be unique and interesting, whilst at the same time reflecting your products, your own personality and what appeals to your target market.

Choosing your business colours should also take you some time. I chose mine from my bunny's dress and fur back in 2009 when I started Bustle & Sew. I didn't know too much about branding then and was lucky that my choices worked out well! Be sure that you carry your colours throughout your business - including your website, business cards and packaging. Think again about the Coca-Cola red and white with its distinctive font - you know whose product you're seeing without ever having to read the name. Take plenty of time to develop your brand identity as you will live and work with it every day - hopefully for a very long time! Changing your mind further down the line could be very expensive - and confusing for your customers too - so work hard to get it right first time.

Once you've created your brand, then you will need to protect it. Thinking of Coca-Cola again - your brand is possibly the most important business asset you possess. The world of intellectual property and copyright is a very complex one with laws that vary from country to country so you should always take legal advice wherever you live. In the UK we have four main kinds of intellectual property that can be protected - patents, trademarks, designs and copyright.

Patents These are essentially what make a thing work, eg what makes a wheel turn, or the chemical formula of your favourite fizzy drink. Trademarks These are signs like words and logos that distinguish goods and services in the marketplace. I have protected my Bustle & Sew bunny logo with a trademark. Design What a logo or product looks like - from the shape of an aeroplane to a fashion item. Copyright An automatic right that comes into existence for anything written or recorded.

It's important to understand the difference between these types of intellectual property and there will be government websites in your own country to help you. If you're in the UK then visit the Intellectual Property Office website www.ipo.gov.uk.

Remember - your brand is your promise to your customers and it's important that you remain true to it. Customers won't return to you - or recommend your products to others - if you don't deliver on your promises.

Very often your packaged items will be your customers' first physical encounter with your business, whether you're sending your work online or directly through, for example, a craft fair. As we discussed above, packaging forms an important part of your business branding, but that doesn't mean it has to be expensive or complicated.

Choose packaging that reflects your business credentials. For example, if you are proud to be environmentally friendly, repurposing and recycling the materials you use to make your products, you might like to think about wrapping them in recycled paper or even left over pieces of fabric you can't use elsewhere. Finish off with a tag (incorporating your logo and business details of course!) and you'll have a lovely eye-catching parcel to give or send to your customer. Again - if you're posting think about strength, durability and cost of posting your items - here in the UK sending a boxed item tends to be more expensive than the same item in a padded envelope (assuming it fits of course!). You could even use recycled packaging - but be sure to brand it with your own stickers and labels - and tell your customers what you're doing and why.

Packaging doesn't have to be expensive - after all it all adds to your overheads, but some careful thought and a little love will bring you dividends. Everyone loves receiving a beautifully packaged items - so think about simple but effective ideas such as wrapping in tissue paper and string or ribbon in colours to match your branding. This is a cost-effective idea but also rather lovely. Consider also including a handwritten note to emphasise the unique handcrafted nature of your items and make shopping with you a very personal, and pleasurable experience.

I hope you're enjoying this series on Making Money from Making. I'll be back next month with more tips - this time looking at marketing your products. After all, it's no good having the loveliest items in the world if nobody knows about them!

Take care when packaging your products.

Vintage schoolroom poster from the 1950's

Bustle & Sew

Love to Sew and Sew with Love .....

Whoops! Bunny Skittles

I originally created these bunny skittles way back in autumn 2011 for issue 11 of the magazine. I've always loved them and thought it would be fun to revist them a massive 28 issues (more than 2 years!) later. This time round I've simplified their construction - just hinting at their features and given them homemade woolly pompom tails. I've also included my original instructions for their storage tub. Bunnies stand approx 10" tall to the tips of their ears.

To make one bunny you will need:

- 10" square medium weight (eg Cath Kidston cotton duck) patterned fabric

- 5" square contrasting felt for inner ears and base

- Stranded cotton floss for cross stitching around ears

- 3" square cardboard

- ¼" button for nose

- Cream or white yarn for tail

- Toy stuffing

- Smooth round pebble to weight base (optional)

Make your bunny:

- Cut one body shape and two outer ears from main fabric, two inner ears and base from felt. Then cut a slightly smaller base circle from cardboard.

- Fold your body shape in half vertically with right sides together and machine stitch from

the back of the head to the base using a ¼" seam allowance. Clip curves, turn right side out and press.

- Stuff bunny shape, inserting pebble wrapped in toy stuffing at the bottom. Join felt base with cross stitch, working half cross stitch in one direction, then back again to complete the stitch. When you're half way round insert the cardboard base and add any additional stuffing to make your bunny's body nice and firm.

- Place felt inner and fabric outer ear shapes wrong sides together and stitch around edge with cross stitch using 2 strands of cotton embroidery floss.

- Fold ears in half and stitch to sides of head. Add small button for nose.

- Make pompom from yarn - there are some great tutorials online if you don't know how to do this - try Makeithandmade… http://www.makeithandmade.com/2012/12/perfect-pom-pom-tutorial.html

- Stitch to body at rear base.

- Your bunny is now finished!

As I mentioned before, my bunnies have seen several incarnations - here they are made in felted woollens and given eyes and whiskers too!

I've also made a storage tub for them - the template for the sitting bunny is included on the templates page, and if you'd like to make your own bunny storage, here's how to do it.

You will need:

- 35" x 8" piece of canvas for lining

- 11" circle of canvas for base

- 10" circle of medium to heavy weight card for base.

- 35" x 3 ½" piece of green fabric

- 11" circle of green fabric for base

- 35" x 4 ½" piece of blue or blue mix fabric

- 35" x 2 ½" piece of cream or cream mix fabric

- Seven 6" x 3" pieces of felt or other fabric for bunnies' bodies.

- Tiny scraps of red and white felt for toadstools

- Cream, green and black stranded cotton floss

- Bondaweb

- Embroidery foot for sewing machine

Seam allowance is ¼"

Make your tub:

- Join your green, blue and cream strips of fabric along the long edges. Press seams flat. This makes the outside of the tub

- Trace 7 bunny shapes onto the paper side of your bondaweb, cut out roughly, then fuse to reverse of fabric. Cut out along lines with nice smooth cuts, then position your shapes on the outside of the tub as shown in the diagram below (not to scale)

- When you're happy with the position of your bunnies then fuse into place protecting your fabric with a cloth if necessary.

- Drop the feed dogs on your sewing machine and fit the embroidery foot. Machine applique into place using dark thread in your needle and lighter colour in your bobbin (this prevents the line looking too hard and solid) Go around each bunny twice for a "scribble" effect.

- Stitch tails with cream floss and French knots – or if preferred you could use a small circle of white felt.

- Add whiskers and scatter a few tiny felt toadstools – the stems are just tiny rectangles and the tops semi-circles or elongated semi-circles. Work some grass around the toadstools in green floss.

- When your applique is finished press lightly on the reverse, then join the two short sides.

- Insert the 11" circle of green fabric as your base. Clip around the edges (but watch you don't snip your stitches!) Turn ¼" cream fabric to inside and press firmly. Then turn ¾" over and press again.
- Make the lining by joining the two short edges of your inner fabric and inserting the 11" circle as the base.
- Insert card circle into base of outer, then insert lining into outer, wrong sides together
- Tuck the top edge under the turned over part of cream fabric, then slip stitch into place.
- Finished!!

My original bunnies - I gave them patchwork tummies (cut from the same circle as the base), whiskers and eyes. I also used smaller, ready-made pompoms, but now much prefer to make my own.

If making for a child you could give yours patchwork tummies too and maybe applique numbers or letters to them (eg a name) for extra personality. These bunnies would be good to make for sale too as they're so quick and easy.

Spring - an Eggstra-ordinary season!

All around there are signs of a fresh year getting under way as the first flowers of spring are blooming in the hedgerows and the fickle English weather warms us with sunshine one moment and throws showers of freezing rain at us the next! This is a good time to organise your shelves and store cupboards which will soon begin to fill up again once spring shades into early summer and the hedgerows, fields and your garden begin to produce their annual harvest.

Eggs have always been a token of spring and the purity of their shape never fails to please. Piled into a bowl or basket in your kitchen they suggest the pleasures to come - of cakes, sauces, meringues (of course!) and lovely fruit curds.

They are the first foods of the new season to become available and our chickens, ducks and geese begin to lay in earnest. To this day they remain a symbol of the season and of re-birth (especially at Easter time) and though we now buy our eggs from the supermarket all year round, people who keep chickens (like my lovely neighbour Belinda, whose hens I can hear happily clucking from my summerhouse) still have a spring glut of fresh, delicious eggs to deal with.

At one time hens laid eggs mainly during the spring months, with geese and ducks laying only at that time, so many methods of preservation were devised to keep the spring glut available for the barren months of the year.

Eggs were individually painted with grease or zinc ointment, or kept under limewater or waterglass. Special galvanised buckets with lids were available for this purpose, with a removable wire basket inside to hold the eggs.

Another method of preservation was simply to rub butter all over the shells, or submerge them in a mixture of salt, water, slaked lime and cream of tartar. Eggshells are naturally porous and all these processes aimed to block that porosity, preventing bacteria from entering the egg and spoiling the contents.

Nowadays we still don't have a means of keeping eggs perfectly fresh, and even the freezer doesn't really help though you can separate the yolks from the white and freeze them for later cake making. Whole beaten eggs can also be frozen, but again are only good for cakes and omelettes - and never quite as nice as using fresh ones.

It's far better to use a glut of eggs in a quite different way by making special, possibly slightly luxurious things that will keep for at least some time and are always welcome additions. Lemon and other fruit curds are a good example as the abundance of eggs coincides perfectly with lemons in season. Other ideas might include cakes or biscuits such as macaroons and meringues. Yum!

Woodland Alphabet Quilt

Made with love for friends of mine who will be adopting a baby later this spring. It's a little boy - and so I created this quilt design for him - though it would be nice for girls too of course!

Finished quilt measures 34" x 48" (approx) after washing.

- The applique shapes are secured to the background fabric with a short machine zig-zag stitch with invisible thread in the needle.

- The animal cheeks are tiny circles of pink felt cut and applied in the same way.

- Use 2 strands of embroidery floss throughout. The handstitched details are worked after the applique shapes have been machine stitched.

Below are photos of individual picture blocks with notes on working where appropriate:

You will need:

- Twelve 10" x 8" rectangles of white cotton fabric

- Lots of fabric scraps for applique and for joining together to make sashing.

- Pink felt

- Stranded cotton floss in gold, black and pink

- Bondaweb

- ½ yard border fabric

- 40" x 54" batting

- 40" x 54" backing fabric

- Invisible thread

Applique panels:

- All the templates are given actual size. Trace the shapes onto the paper side of your bondaweb, cut out roughly and then fuse to the reverse of your scrap. Cut out the shape carefully using long smooth strokes and position on your backing fabric. Do not fuse until you are happy with their positioning.

- When building up shapes, start from the bottom and work upwards, eg first fuse the hedgehog body before adding his prickles.

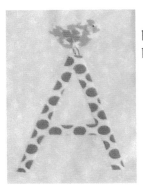

Bird eye is a tiny stitch of black floss and legs are backstitched.

Cut the body shape in a dark fabric first, then the lighter grey back and finally the lightest grey for the face markings. The cheek is positioned over the edge of the face marking. The nose and eye are hand stitched in black.

Cut and apply the main body up to the neck (allow extra to underlap). Then cut the head shape in lighter fabric - scooping down between ears. Finally cut the brown head shape and apply on top of the lighter fabric. Cheeks, eyes and nose as before.

Cut and apply hedgehog main body first, then prickles. Nose, eye and cheek as before.

First cut and apply the back leg, allowing extra for it to be overlapped by the tummy. Then cut the tummy and tail as one piece and apply. Finally the main rabbit body. Cheek, eye and nose as before.

First apply the tree foliage, then the trunk and finally the letter "I" sitting on top of the trunk shape.

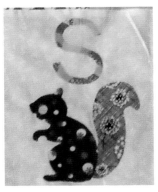

Cut and apply the tail first, allowing extra for the base to be overlapped by the main body piece. Eye, cheek and nose as before.

Apply the mouse body and then the head. Ears and tail are back stitch in pale pink floss. Eyes, nose and cheeks as before.

Take some time choosing your fabric scraps, and try to incorporate the same pieces in more than one panel to give a harmonious feeling. Keep to the same colour palette for your sashing.

Assembling your quilt:

When finished, press your applique blocks on the reverse. I created my sashing strips by joining more scraps, but you could use fabric if you preferred.

Use a ¼" seam allowance throughout.

You will need:

- Eight 10" x 2" strips to join your blocks horizontally

- Three 26" x 2" strips to join your panels vertically.

- Two 26" x 4" border strips for top and bottom

- Two 46" x 6" border strips for sides

Apply the main body shape, then the chest. The spectacles and beak fall on top of the chest and all are secured with machine zig-zag. The "O" is positioned in the middle of the chest. The eyes are blanket stitch worked in black floss.

44

- Join your applique blocks in four rows of three using the eight 10" x 2" strips between them.

- Join these rows vertically, separating with the longer sashing strips.

- Press on reverse

- Add borders to top, bottom and sides of quilt.

- Your quilt top is now complete.

Finishing your quilt:

I used a light weight cotton batting with 3% shrinkage and quilted the quilt all over with a random stipple pattern with invisible thread in my needle to avoid obscuring the applique designs. I finished by binding in the same fabric as the borders.

Pattern Templates

Cottage Gardens Templates

Actual size and reversed for tracing onto Bondaweb.

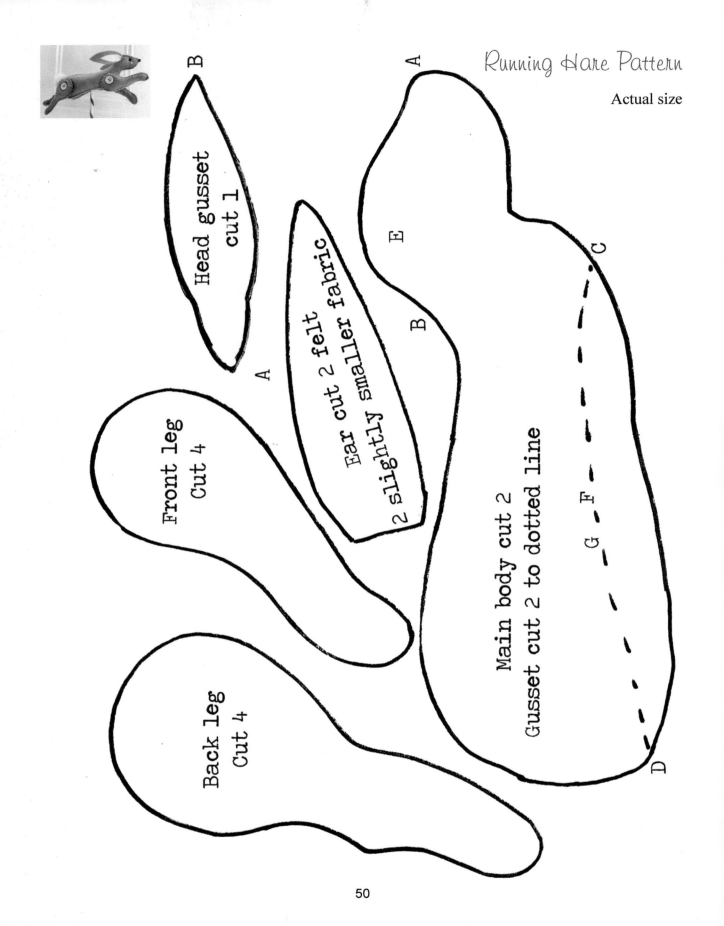

Actual size

B

Head gusset
cut 1

A

A

E

B

C

Ear cut 2 felt
slightly smaller fabric
2 slightly smaller

Front leg
Cut 4

Main body cut 2
Gusset cut 2 to dotted line

G F

Back leg
Cut 4

D

Digging the Allotment

Actual size

Country Houses Bunting Template Actual size

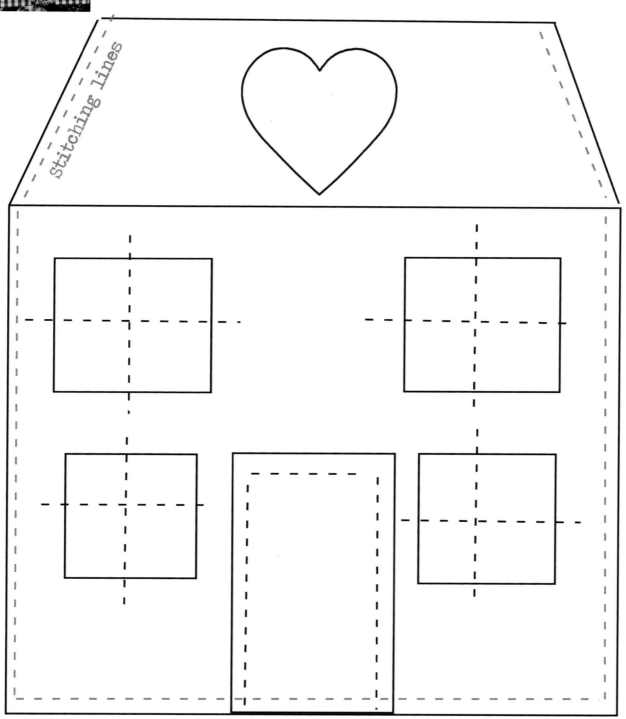

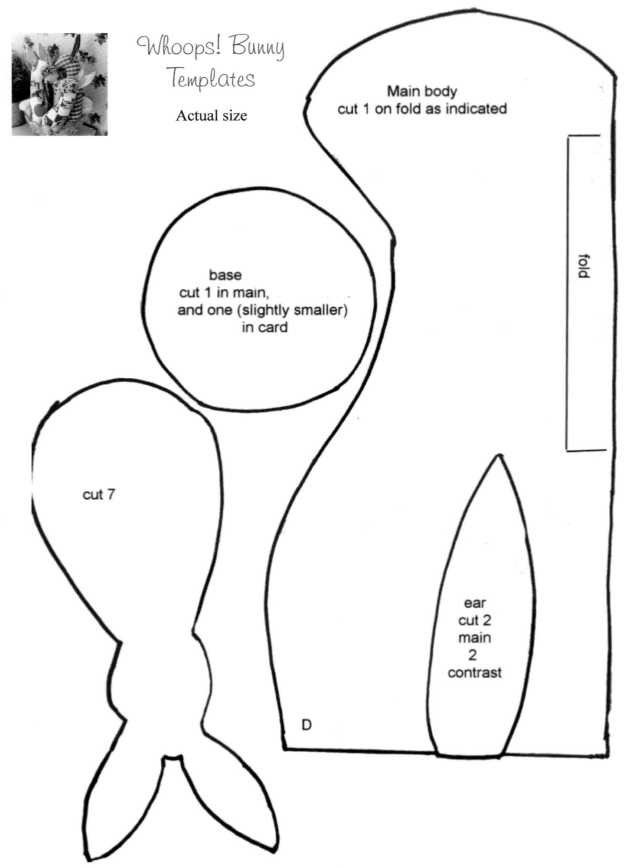

Whoops! Bunny
Templates

Actual size

Main body
cut 1 on fold as indicated

fold

base
cut 1 in main,
and one (slightly smaller)
in card

cut 7

ear
cut 2
main
2
contrast

D

Woodland Alphabet Quilt Templates

Actual size and reversed for tracing onto Bondaweb

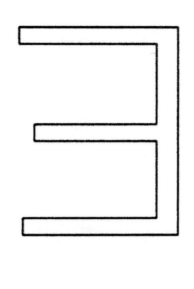

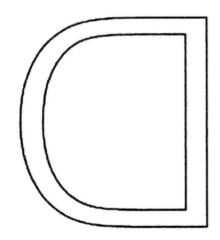

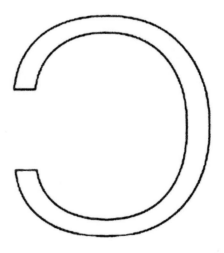

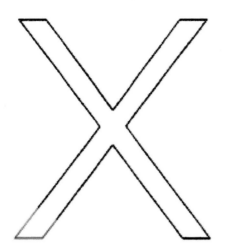

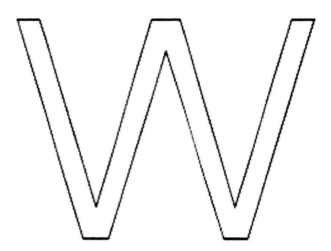

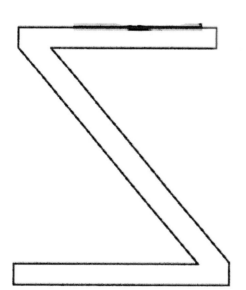

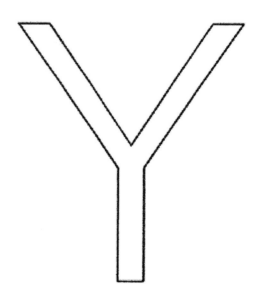

Printed in Great Britain
by Amazon.co.uk, Ltd.,
Marston Gate.